WIPE-CLEAN LEARNING

Early
ENGLISH

A-Z

AUTUMN
PUBLISHING

Aa is for apple

Trace the words.

ants

arm

anteater

aliens

airplane

Write two words beginning with a.

 ....

Draw a picture of something beginning with a and write what it is next to it.

Complete the sentence by tracing the a words.

An ant arrived at **the** anthill **to eat** an apple.

Write your own sentence using an a word. Remember to use a capital letter at the start of your sentence, and a period at the end.

....

....

B b is for book

Trace the words.

ball

baby

boat

bird

banana

Write two words beginning with **b**.

....

....

Draw a picture of something beginning with **b** and write what it is next to it.

Complete the sentence by tracing the **b** words.

Bear **read a** blue book **about** bats.

Write your own sentence using a **b** word. Remember to use a capital letter at the start of your sentence, and a period at the end.

....

....

C c is for cat

Trace the words.

cat

chair

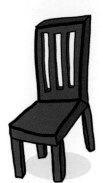

coins

cake

cow

Write two words beginning with c.

....

....

Draw a picture of something beginning with **c** and write what it is next to it.

Complete the sentence by tracing the **c** words.

The cute cat curled up close to the chair.

Write your own sentence using a **c** word. Remember to use a capital letter at the start of your sentence, and a period at the end.

....

....

D d is for dog

Trace the words.

dog

duck

doctor

dress

drink

Write two words beginning with **d**.

....

....

Draw a picture of something beginning with **d** and write what it is next to it.

Complete the sentence by tracing the **d** words.

The dog and donkey dashed to the duck pond.

Write your own sentence using a **d** word. Remember to use a capital letter at the start of your sentence, and a period at the end.

  is for

E **e** is for egg

Trace the words.

 ear  envelope

 elephant

 Earth emoji

Write two words beginning with **e**.

 ....

Draw a picture of something beginning with **e** and write what it is next to it.

Complete the sentence by tracing the e words.

The elephant found an

enormous emu egg.

Write your own sentence using an **e** word. Remember to use a capital letter at the start of your sentence, and a period at the end.

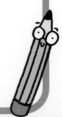

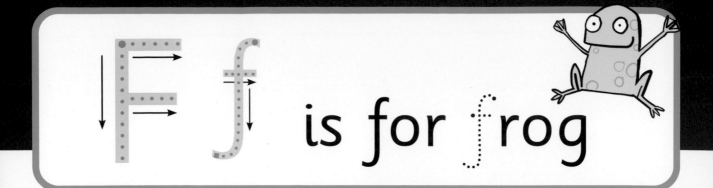

F f is for frog

Trace the words.

 frog

flower

fishing

 fish

 fox

Write two words beginning with f.

  ....

  ....

Draw a picture of something beginning with **f** and write what it is next to it.

Complete the sentence by tracing the **f** words.

The frog hopped through the flowers in the forest.

Write your own sentence using an **f** word. Remember to use a capital letter at the start of your sentence, and a period at the end.

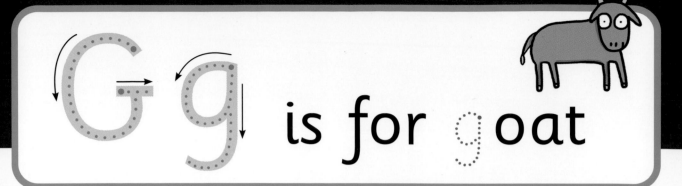

G g is for goat

Trace the words.

girl

glass

giraffe

grass

globe

Write two words beginning with g.

....

....

Draw a picture of something beginning with **g** and write what it is next to it.

Complete the sentence by tracing the **g** words.

The gray goat loved green grapes.

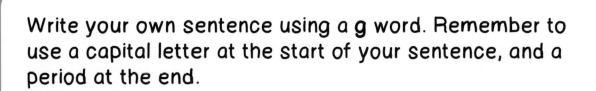

Write your own sentence using a **g** word. Remember to use a capital letter at the start of your sentence, and a period at the end.

Hh is for hay

Trace the words.

 horse

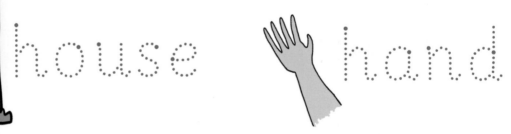 hill

hamburger

house

hand

Write two words beginning with **h**.

 ....

 ....

Draw a picture of something beginning with h and write what it is next to it.

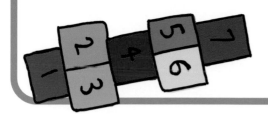

Complete the sentence by tracing the h words.

The haunted house was halfway up the hill.

Write your own sentence using an h word. Remember to use a capital letter at the start of your sentence, and a period at the end.

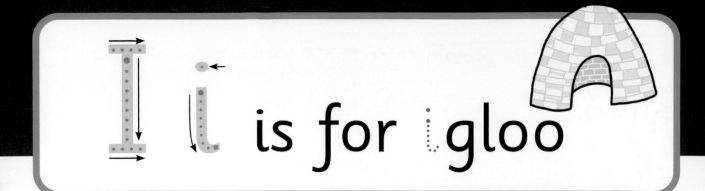

I i is for igloo

Trace the words.

 icicle

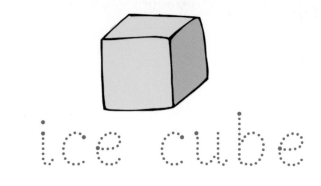 ice cube

 insect

 island

 ink

Write two words beginning with i.

 ....

Draw a picture of something beginning with i and write what it is next to it.

Complete the sentence by tracing the i words.

The insect was interested in the invention.

Write your own sentence using an i word. Remember to use a capital letter at the start of your sentence, and a period at the end.

J j is for jelly

Trace the words.

jaguar

jar

jellyfish

jump

juice

Write two words beginning with j.

....

....

Draw a picture of something beginning with j and write what it is next to it.

Complete the sentence by tracing the j words.

The jaguar told

jokes to the jellyfish.

Write your own sentence using a j word. Remember to use a capital letter at the start of your sentence, and a period at the end.

....

....

K k is for kite

Trace the words.

 king

 kitten

 kangaroo

 knife

 knight

---

Write two words beginning with **k**.

....

Draw a picture of something beginning with **k**
and write what it is next to it.

Complete the sentence by tracing the **k** words.

The kangaroo kicked the kite.

Write your own sentence using a **k** word. Remember to use a capital letter at the start of your sentence, and a period at the end.

....

....

L l is for lemon

Trace the words.

light ladybug

lily pad

 lemon  lion

Write two words beginning with l.

....

Draw a picture of something beginning with I and write what it is next to it.

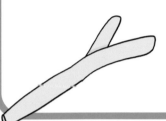

Complete the sentence by tracing the I words.

The little lemur liked green leaves.

Write your own sentence using an I word. Remember to use a capital letter at the start of your sentence, and a period at the end.

?

Mm is for map

Trace the words.

 meat

medal

 monster

 mice

 mop

Write two words beginning with **m**.

 ....

 ....

Draw a picture of something beginning with **m** and write what it is next to it.

Complete the sentence by tracing the **m** words.

The mechanic made **a big** mess.

Write your own sentence using an **m** word. Remember to use a capital letter at the start of your sentence, and a period at the end.

....

....

N n is for notes

Trace the words.

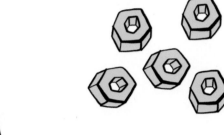

nuts

newspaper

notepad

Write two words beginning with **n**.

Draw a picture of something beginning with **n** and write what it is next to it.

Complete the sentence by tracing the **n** words.

The bird nest was cozy at night.

Write your own sentence using an **n** word. Remember to use a capital letter at the start of your sentence, and a period at the end.

....

....

O o is for octopus

Trace the words.

owl

octopus

octagon

Write two words beginning with o.

 ....  ....

Draw a picture of something beginning with **o** and write what it is next to it.

Complete the sentence by tracing the **o** words.

The orange octopus waved at the old owl.

Write your own sentence using an **o** word. Remember to use a capital letter at the start of your sentence, and a period at the end.

....

....

P p is for penguin

Trace the words.

pigeon

painting

peas

Write two words beginning with p.

   ....

   ....

Draw a picture of something beginning with **p** and write what it is next to it.

Complete the sentence by tracing the **p** words.

The pirate ate pears and pineapples.

Write your own sentence using a **p** word. Remember to use a capital letter at the start of your sentence, and a period at the end.

....

....

 **Q q is for q ueen**

Trace the words.

queen

quill

quarter

Write two words beginning with **q**.

 . . . .  . . . .

Draw a picture of something beginning with q and write what it is next to it.

Complete the sentence by tracing the q words.

The queen questioned the quilt on her bed.

Write your own sentence using a q word. Remember to use a capital letter at the start of your sentence, and a period at the end.

....

....

R r is for robot

Trace the words.

racecar

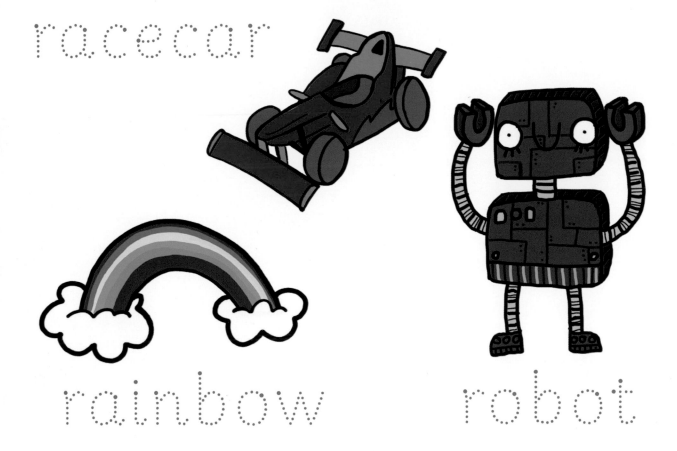

rainbow   robot

Write two words beginning with r.

....

Draw a picture of something beginning with r and write what it is next to it.

Complete the sentence by tracing the r words.

The red rocket soared over the rainbow.

Write your own sentence using an r word. Remember to use a capital letter at the start of your sentence, and a period at the end.

....

....

S s is for sun

Trace the words.

seal

spider

sheep

Complete the sentence by tracing the **s** words.

The snail ate the strawberry.

Write your own sentence using an **s** word. Remember to use a capital letter at the start of your sentence, and a period at the end.

....

....

T t is for tractor

Trace the words.

triceratops

tortoise

flashlight

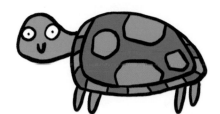

Complete the sentence by tracing the t words.

The turtle won the trophy.

Write your own sentence using a t word. Remember to use a capital letter at the start of your sentence, and a period at the end.

....

....

U u is for unicorn

Trace the words.

unicorn

umbrella

unhappy

Complete the sentence by tracing the u words.

The uncle rode the unicycle.

Write your own sentence using a u word.
Remember to use a capital letter at the start of
your sentence, and a period at the end.

....

....

Vv is for violin

Trace the words.

van

vet

Complete the sentence by tracing the v words.

The vulture loved vegetables.

Write your own sentence using a v word. Remember to use a capital letter at the start of your sentence, and a period at the end.

....

....

W w is for water

Trace the words.

witch

wand

whale

Complete the sentence by tracing the **w** words.

The wiggly worm was wet.

Write your own sentence using a **w** word. Remember to use a capital letter at the start of your sentence, and a period at the end.

....

....

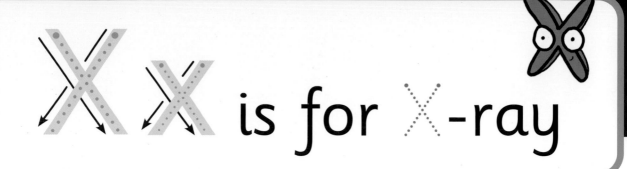

X x is for X-ray

Trace the words.

xylophone

X-ray

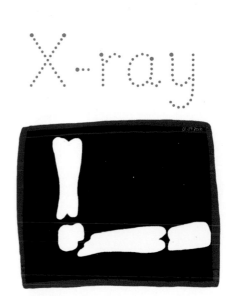

Complete the sentence by tracing the x words.

Xavier **played the** xylophone.

Write your own sentence using an x word. Remember to use a capital letter at the start of your sentence, and a period at the end.

Y y is for yo-yo

Trace the words.

yacht

yolk

yo-yo

Complete the sentence by tracing the **y** words.

The yo-yo was yellow.

Write your own sentence using a **y** word. Remember to use a capital letter at the start of your sentence, and a period at the end.

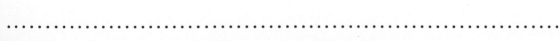

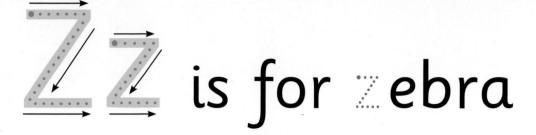 **Zz** is for zebra

Trace the words.

zipper

zebra

zookeeper

Complete the sentence by tracing the z words.

The zookeeper fed the zebra.

Write your own sentence using a z word. Remember to use a capital letter at the start of your sentence, and a period at the end.

....

....

WIPE-CLEAN LEARNING

Give your child a head start at school with this big book of games and activities, reviewed by educational experts. Then wipe the pages clean and play all over again!

AUTUMN
PUBLISHING

autumnpublishing.co.uk

First published in the UK by Autumn Publishing
An imprint of Igloo Books Ltd
Cottage Farm, NN6 0BJ, UK
Owned by Bonnier Books
Sveavägen 56, Stockholm, Sweden
All rights reserved, including the right of
reproduction in whole or in part in any form.
Educational consultant: Carrie Lewis
Illustrated by Katie Abey
Designed by Lee Italiano
Edited by Rebecca Kealy
Manufactured in China. 0423 001
10 9 8 7 6 5 4 3 2 1

US $8.99
CAN $11.99

Conforms to ASTM D4236

Climate Neutral Product

3+

⚠ **WARNING:**
CHOKING HAZARD – Small parts.
Not for children under 3 yrs.

ISBN 978-1-83852-787-7

50899

9 781838 527877